HOW PETE SEEGER GOT AMERICA SINGING

LISTEN

Leda
Schubert

Pictures by
Raúl Colón

A NEAL PORTER BOOK
Roaring Brook Press   New York

Listen.

There was nobody like Pete Seeger.

Wherever he went, he got people singing.

With his head thrown back

and his Adam's apple bouncing,

picking his long-necked banjo

or strumming his twelve-string guitar,

Pete sang old songs,

new songs,

old songs with new words,

and songs he made up.

In front of crowds large and small, he'd raise his arm.
"Basses, here's your part," he'd say.
"Tenors, sopranos, altos, here's yours."
Four-part harmony would rise to the rafters
and drift to the stars.
"Participation. That's what's gonna save the human race."

Listen.

Pete participated his whole life.

He led marches to end wars;

he stood on peace lines in cold and snow, heat and rain.

"Down by the Riverside." "Where Have All the Flowers Gone?"

He joined rallies to support the work of unions.

"Which Side Are You On?" "Joe Hill." "Union Maid."

He sang ballads, blues, and love songs.

"The Water Is Wide." "Come All Ye Fair and Tender Ladies."

"Shenandoah."

But that's not all.

Pete loved singing with children,

and children loved singing with Pete.

Thousands sang with him.

"Abiyoyo." "Froggie Went a-Courting." "Skip to My Lou."

Pete and his good friend Woody Guthrie
traveled the country making up songs.
They sang with hoboes, union organizers, and farmers;
they hopped freight trains
and they kept singing.
"Hard Travellin'." "This Land Is Your Land." "Pastures of Plenty."

Pete, Woody, and friends

formed the Almanac Singers.

Then Pete joined the Weavers,

who became very famous indeed.

They had a number-one hit with "Goodnight, Irene,"

a song they learned from Lead Belly,

and hundreds of thousands sang with them.

"Tzena, Tzena, Tzena." "When the Saints Go Marching In."

"Wimoweh."

At just about that time, Pete got into trouble.

What trouble?

This trouble:

The House Un-American Activities Committee

of the United States Congress

questioned whether Pete was a true American.

Pete said, "I love my country very deeply,"

offered to sing a song,

and stood by his First Amendment right,

the right of free speech.

"Wasn't That a Time?" "Guantanamera."

He was indicted for contempt of Congress.